CONTENTS

Author: **Janet Monseu**

Editor-in-Chief: Richard W. Wheeler, M.A.Ed.

Editor: Jane Snow-Peterson

Consulting Editor: Howard Stitt, Th.M., Ed.D.

Revision Editor: Alan Christopherson, M.S.

Alpha Omega Publications®

804 N. 2nd Ave. E., Rock Rapids, IA 51246-1759

Learn with our friends:

When you see me, I will help your teacher explain the exciting things you are expected to do.

When you do actions with me, you will learn how to write, draw, match words, read, and much more.

You and I will learn about matching words, listening, drawing, and other fun things in your lessons.

History & Geography
Student Book

Grade **3**
Unit **7**

Alpha Omega Publications®

COAL MINING AND PENNSYLVANIA

In this LIFEPAC® you will learn about coal mining in Pennsylvania. First, you will study about how coal was formed long ago and why coal is important today. Next, you will read about early coal mining and mining today. You will share a boy's exciting adventure in a mining community in Pennsylvania. Then you will learn about Pennsylvania, the state where coal mining is an important way of making a living.

 **Objectives**

Read these objectives. They will tell you what you will be able to do when you have finished this LIFEPAC.

1. You will be able to explain how coal was formed.
2. You will be able to name two kinds of coal.
3. You will be able to describe the early ways of mining.
4. You will be able to name three ways mining has changed over the years.
5. You will be able to tell why coal is important to people.
6. You will be able to write five facts about Pennsylvania.

NEW WORDS

anthracite coal (an' thru sīt kōl). Hard coal.

bifocal (bī'fō kul). Glasses worn by people who need two different ways to see.

bituminous coal (bu tü' mu nus kōl). Soft coal.

by-product (bī' prod' ukt). Something made from leftover products.

charcoal (chär' kōl). Partly burned wood.

concrete (kon krēt). Broken stone mixed with sand, water, and cement.

energy (en' ur jē). Power; the strength to do something.

explosion (ek splō' zhun). Blowing up with a loud noise.

explosive (ek splō' siv). Something that causes an explosion.

factory (fak' tur ē). A place where things are made.

fertilizer (fėr' tu lī zur). Product that enriches the soil.

fuel (fyü ul). Anything that burns.

hoist (hoist). To lift up.

mining (mī' ning). Digging out minerals from the ground.

oxygen (ok' su jun). The gas which people breathe in order to live.

peat (pēt). A softer, early form of coal.

product (prod' ukt). Something that is made from something else; the result of work.

prop (prop). A support to hold up something.

rescue (res' kyü). Save from danger.

seam (sēm). A layer of coal.

shaft mining (shaft mī′ ning). Mining done under the ground.

steel (stēl). A mixture of carbon and iron that is very hard and strong.

strip mining (strip mī′ ning). Mining done on the surface of the ground.

surface (sėr′ fis). The top of something.

swamp (swomp). Wet, muddy land.

tar (tär). A thick, dark-colored, oily material.

tipple (tip′ ul). The building where the coal is loaded onto railroad cars or trucks.

These words will appear in **boldface** (darker print) the first time they are used.

Pronunciation Key: hat, āge, cãre, fär; let, ēqual, tėrm; it, īce; hot, ōpen, ôrder; oil; out; cup, pút, rüle; child; long; thin; /ᴛH/ for then; /zh/ for measure; /u/ represents /a/ in about, /e/ in taken, /o/ in lemon, and /u/ in circus.

I. FACTS ABOUT COAL

Coal is a **fuel** that burns slowly and provides warmth for people and **energy** for running machines. Coal has been used for hundreds of years. A large supply of coal lies under the ground in the United States.

anthracite coal	(an′ thru sīt kōl)	Hard coal.
bituminous coal	(bu tü′ mu nus kōl)	Soft coal.

by-product	(bī′ prod′ ukt)	Something made from leftover products.
charcoal	(chär′ kōl)	Partly burned wood.
energy	(en′ ur jē)	Power; the strength to do something.
factory	(fak′tur ē)	A place where things are made.
fertilizer	(fėr′ tu lī zur)	Product that enriches the soil.
fuel	(fyü′ ul)	Anything that burns.
peat	(pēt)	A softer, early form of coal.
product	(prod′ ukt)	Something that is made from something else; the result of work.
swamp	(swomp)	Wet, muddy land.
tar	(tär)	A thick, dark-colored, oily material.

Ask your teacher to say these words with you.
Teacher check _____

                          Initial   Date

FORMATION OF COAL

A long time ago coal started to form from dead trees and plants. The trees and plants fell into **swamps.** As the plants lay in the swamps, **peat** was formed.

Peat is moist and spongy with many little plants in it. Peat is more like wood than coal. When peat is dug up and dried out, it will burn slowly.

In some places peat can be found today. In other places the water has been pressed out by the weight of the soil now on top of the peat. Over many years, coal has formed from the peat.

Do this activity.

The sentences tell what happens when coal is formed. The sentences are not in the right order.

1.1   Number the sentences correctly 1, 2, 3, 4, and 5. Then rewrite the sentences on these lines.

a. _____ Soil presses water from peat.

b. _____ Dead trees and plants fall into swamps.

c. _____ Coal was formed from peat.

d. _____ Dead trees and plants were the beginnings of coal.

e. _____ A wet, wood-like peat formed from dead trees and plants.

_____

_____

_____

_____

_____

_____

_____

_____

IMPORTANCE OF COAL

Everything that moves or works needs **energy.**

Your body needs energy so that you can work and play. Food is used to make energy for your body.

Machines also need energy if they are to work for people. **Fuel** is used to make machines work.

Coal is important because coal is a fuel. Coal can be used to make energy to run machines in **factories.**

You know about many things used for fuel. You burn **charcoal** in your outdoor grill. A car engine burns gasoline. Paper and wood can be used for fuel. However, coal is a good fuel because coal burns for a longer time.

Since coal is a good fuel, coal is very important to the world.

 **Fill in the missing letters of the words.**

1.2   These words name some fuels. The missing letters spell another fuel.

C H A R ____ O A L

W ____ O D

P ____ P E R

G A S O ____ I N E

Read these words.

1.3   Circle the words that name fuels.

oil   sand   water   twigs
  gasoline   rocks   hay
air   glass   straw   newspaper

TYPES OF COAL

Coal was formed in the earth when rock layers pressed the plants into a new form. Different kinds of coal were formed. The first coal formed was soft. Coal that was pressed longer became hard.

Bituminous coal is soft coal. A soft coal burns more quickly and easily than harder coal. When

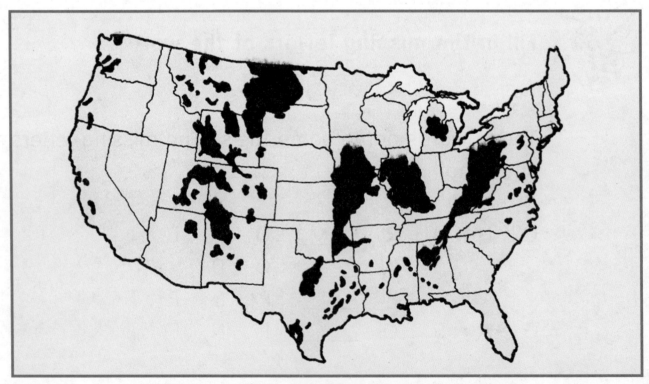

Coal Supplies Of The United States

bituminous coal burns, a yellow flame and smoke are given off. Burning bituminous coal makes a very hot fire. Bituminous coal is burned in factories to make energy to run machines. Bituminous coal is found in western Pennsylvania and in other parts of our country. The United States has a good supply of bituminous coal.

Anthracite coal is the hardest, blackest coal. It burns for a long time. Anthracite coal burns with very little smoke or flame. Very little anthracite coal is found in the world. In the United States it is found only in eastern Pennsylvania.

Do this reading activity.

> A piece of coal will burn. Reread the first sentence. Listen when you say the word piece. You say a long /ē/ sound for the letters ie. Usually this long /ē/ sound is spelled ie. When the sound follows the letter c, the sound is spelled ei. It is easy to remember if you say: "i before e except after c."

1.4 **Spell the following words correctly**. Put in either ie or ei for the long /e/ sound.

a. bel ___ ___ve

b. p ___ ___ce

c. rec ___ ___ve

d. c ___ ___ling

e. f ___ ___ld

f. n ___ ___ce

g. ch ___ ___f

Use the words you spelled to fill the blanks in these sentences.

1.5   We _____ God gave us a beautiful earth to enjoy.

1.6   A _____ of bituminous coal burns more quickly than hard coal.

1.7   Your girl cousin is your father's _____ .

1.8   The factory will _____ the coal today.

1.9   The _____ of the room is painted white.

1.10   The farmer planted corn in his _____ .

1.11   The Indian _____ called coal "black rocks that burn."

After each sentence, write either the word anthracite **or** bituminous **to tell what kind of coal the phrase is describing.**

1.12   The hardest, blackest coal. _____

1.13   A soft coal. _____

1.14   Very little of this kind of coal in the world.

           _____

1.15   In our country this coal is found only in Pennsylvania. _____

1.16   Makes a very hot fire. _____

1.17   Will burn for a long time. _____

1.18   Burns quickly and easily because it is soft. _____

BY-PRODUCTS OF COAL

Besides being an important fuel, coal has many **by-products**. When coal is burned, heat is a by-product. Gases and **tars** are also formed. These gases and tars are used to make other **products**.

Some by-products are man-made rubber, **fertilizers**, medicines, food dyes, and bug sprays.

Not only is coal used for fuel, but also its by-products are used in your life every day.

Some By-Products of Coal

Draw a line to the correct answer.

1.19	spongy beginning of coal	anthracite
1.20	anything that burns	fuel
1.21	hard coal	bituminous
1.22	something made from coal	swamp
1.23	soft coal	peat
1.24	wet land	by-product

For this Self Test, study what you have read and done. The Self Test will check what you remember.

SELF TEST 1

Circle the correct answer.

1.01   Coal is _____.

       a. a plant   b. a fuel   c. slime

1.02   Fuel is used to make _____.

       a. oil   b. factories   c. energy

1.03   A moist, spongy beginning of coal is _____.

       a. ore   b. swamp   c. peat

1.04   A very hard type of coal is _____.

       a. anthracite   b. bituminous   c. peat

1.05   A swamp is _____.

       a. high, dry land   b. wet land   c. a sandpit

Answer in one or two complete sentences. (each answer, 2 points.)

1.06   Tell how coal is formed.

_____

_____

_____

_____

1.07   Why is coal important to people?

_____

_____

Use these words to fill in the blanks.

coal   fuel
by-product   swamps
factories

1.08   Some medicine is a _____ of coal.

1.09   Something that can be burned is a _____.

1.010   Coal began to form when dead trees and plants fell into

_____.

1.011   Energy from burning coal is used in _____ to
run machines.

1.012   Other products can be made when _____ is
burned.

Match the meaning of the words.

1.013   oil, natural gas, coal   soft coal

1.014   energy   anything that burns

1.015   factories   places for making things

1.016   bituminous coal   fuel used to make energy

1.017   fuel   used to run machinery

Circle the correct two answers.

1.018   Peat will _____.

a.   burn   b.   boil   c.   dry out

1.019   Energy is needed to run _____.

a.   our bodies   b.   machines   c.   fuels

1.020   Two types of coal are _____.

a.   generator   b.   bituminous   c.   anthracite

13 (thirteen)

Teacher check _____

Initial   Date

My Score

II. METHODS OF COAL MINING

In the first section of this LIFEPAC, you learned that coal is very useful to people. After people discovered how important coal was, they began **mining** it. In the next section you will learn about coal mining.

VOCABULARY

concrete	(kon' krēt)	Broken stone mixed with sand, water and cement.
explosion	(ek splō' zhun)	Blowing up with a loud noise.
explosive	(ek splō' siv)	Something that causes an explosion.
hoist	(hoist)	To lift up.
mining	(mī' ning)	Digging out minerals from the ground.

oxygen	(ok′ su jun)	The gas that people breathe in order to live.
prop	(prop)	A support to hold up something.
rescue	(res′ kyü)	Save from danger.
seam	(sēm)	A layer of coal.
shaft mining	(shaft mī′ ning)	Mining done under the ground.
steel	(stēl)	A mixture of carbon and iron that is very hard and strong.
strip mining	(strip mī′ ning)	Mining done on the surface of the ground.
surface	(sėr′ fis)	The top of something.
tipple	(tip′ ul)	The building where the coal is loaded onto railroad cars or trucks.

Ask your teacher to say these words with you.
Teacher check _____

Initial   Date

EARLY METHODS

The first mines were only pits dug out of the earth. People climbed down ladders into the narrow pits to get the coal. Next, tunnels were dug to reach more coal.

15 (fifteen)

The coal had to be pulled in baskets back to the pit. Then the coal was **hoisted** to the **surface** of the ground.

Early **mining** was very hard work. Miners used picks to cut the coal from the **seam**. Often the tunnels were not big enough for the miners to stand up straight while they worked. The only light the miners had was from their candles.

The miners, at that time, faced many dangers. As they chipped away at the coal, gas would be found. The flame of a miner's candle could cause the gas to explode. Often, miners were killed by these **explosions**. Coal dust was always in the air and hurt the miners' lungs.

Candles, used for light , also used much of the **oxygen** in the air. The miners needed oxygen to breathe. The poor light also hurt the miner's eyes.

Early Miner at Work

Sometimes the roofs of the mines caved in. The miners working below were killed or trapped. With the shafts blocked, it was hard to **rescue** the trapped miners.

People began to think of ways to make mining a safer way to earn a living.

Many times you can learn the meaning of a word you do not know by reading the sentence in which the new word appears. The way the word is used in the sentence helps you understand what the word means.

In each of these sentences a word is underlined. Read the whole sentence and try to figure out what the underlined word means.

 Write the meaning of the word on the line.

2.1   Mother bought <u>dye</u> to color the faded sheet.

_____

_____

2.2   If you <u>irrigate</u> the land, you will have enough water to grow crops.

_____

_____

2.3   The man was very rich. He had made his <u>fortune</u> mining gold.

_____

_____

2.4   The children put <u>pillars</u> in each corner of their playhouse. The pillars kept the house from falling down.

_____

_____

2.5   God <u>forgives</u> our sins if we ask Him. He no longer holds them against us.

_____

_____

Write true **or** false.

2.6   _____ Early miners used picks to cut coal.
2.7   _____ Flashlights helped miners to see in the mine.
2.8   _____ Mining used to be very dangerous.
2.9   _____ The first mines were pits in the earth.

IMPROVING CONDITIONS

Miners no longer have to carry coal to the surface by hand. Machinery scoops up the coal. The big scoops load the coal into railroad cars that bring it out of the mine.

Miners used to use picks and shovels for their mining tools. Today machines are used to bore holes in the mines. **Explosives** are put in the holes to blast the coal loose.

Now electric lighting is used instead of candles, and fans force fresh air into every part of the mine.

The walls of the mines are held against cave-ins. **Props** of heavy **steel** or **concrete** are built to support the rock above. The safety laws say that a certain amount of coal is to be left in each mine. This coal acts as a natural prop.

A safety lamp was invented that can test for gas in the coal mine. Every mine has a fire boss who goes along all the shafts with the safety lamp to make sure they are safe.

All along the walls of the mines are pipes that carry water to fight fires. Telephones have been put in mines, too. Mining is still hard work, but it is not as dangerous as it once was. Mining is safer today than it was years ago.

Write the words under the right time in mining.

		Years Ago	Today
2.10	candles	_____	_____
2.11	electricity	_____	_____
2.12	picks and shovels	_____	_____
2.13	machines	_____	_____
2.14	explosives	_____	_____
2.15	safety lamps	_____	_____

		Years Ago	Today
2.16	fans	_____	_____
2.17	steel supports	_____	_____
2.18	no supports	_____	_____
2.19	telephones	_____	_____
2.20	no way to call for help	_____	_____
2.21	water lines	_____	_____
2.22	many fires	_____	_____
2.23	many explosions	_____	_____
2.24	many cave-ins	_____	_____
2.25	poor health	_____	_____
2.26	fire boss	_____	_____

MODERN MINING

The mines that used to be small pits are now large enough to have two or more big elevators in them. These elevators are called cages. The cages carry the miners and coal cars between the surface of the earth and the coal below.

The coal is taken out of the mine by railroad cars. After the coal is out of the mine, it is taken into a building. The rocks are taken out of the coal, and the coal is washed. At the **tipple** the coal is loaded on railroad cars or trucks.

HISTORY & GEOGRAPHY

307

LIFEPAC TEST

20/25

Name _____

Date _____

Score _____

HISTORY & GEOGRAPHY 307: LIFEPAC TEST

EACH ANSWER, 1 POINT

Write the correct answer from the word box.

by-product	explosive	gas
swamp	energy	fuel
props	town	work

1. Coal is a _____.

2. The coal in the mine is blasted loose with an

    _____.

3. Fertilizer is a _____ of coal.

4. Wet, muddy land is called a _____.

5. Early mining was hard _____.

6. People and machines can work if they have

    _____.

7. Mine roofs are help up by _____.

8. A fire boss checks for escaping _____in the mine.

9. A coal mine can be as large as a _____.

Number the sentences in order from 1 to 4.

10. _____Dead trees and plants slowly change into peat.

11. _____Trees and plants fall into swamps.

12. _____God makes plants and trees.

13. _____Coal is formed as the peat is pressed into rock.

Circle the correct answer for each sentence.

14. Benjamin Franklin was _____ .
   a. an early miner
   b. a great man in America's history
   c. a king

15. Everything that moves needs _____ .
   a. energy
   b. oxygen
   c. peat

16. William Penn was treating the Indians _____ .
   a. fairly
   b. badly
   c. to a big dinner

17. Mining coal from the surface of the land is called ___.
   a. shaft mining
   b. trenching
   c. strip mining

18. The name of the city which means "brotherly love" is
   _____ .
   a. Pittsburgh
   b. Erie
   c. Philadelphia

19. Fuel makes energy for _____ .
   a. oceans
   b. trees
   c. machines

20. In the story Eric turned for help to _____ .

    a. a policeman

    b. his teacher

    c. God

Write true **or** false.

21. _____ Mining is much safer than it used be.

22. _____ An important part of our country's history happened in Pennsylvania.

23. _____ Peat is the hardest type of coal there is.

24. _____ Benjamin Franklin was a great inventor.

25. _____ Coal is only important to miners.

Today's mine is often the size of a town. Sometimes, the mine may be a much bigger place than the town where the miners live. The tunnels or streets of the mine may go many miles under the earth. Along the streets of the mine are the spaces from which the coal is being mined. This kind of mining is called **shaft mining.** Shaft mining is done deep in the ground.

Modern Mining

The other kind used today is called **strip mining**. Strip mining is used to mine the coal that is close to the top of the ground. Very large machines are used to remove the earth on the surface of the land and then to dig out the layers of coal. Large areas of land are strip mined in this way. Because the miners do not go deep into the ground, strip mining is the safest kind of mining. However, strip mining leaves ugly scars across the land. New laws say that strip mining companies must plant trees and grass on the bare land.

Mining has changed since the days when people first brought coal from the ground. Mining is still a very important way for people to earn their living. Coal is important to people in our country and in the world.

Read these words.

Say the following words: melt, salt, belt. Say the words again and listen for the ending sounds. The ending sounds are the same in all the words.

Write the words from the word box in the right blank.

salt	melt	belt
felt	wilt	built
quilt	halt	

2.27   The miners _____ there should be safety rules in the mine.

2.28   A coal mine is often _____ like a small city.

2.29   A flower will _____ after it is picked.

2.30   The miner carries tools on a_____ around his waist.

2.31   The beautiful patchwork _____ on the bed shows some of the history of early Pennsylvania.

2.32   Ice will _____ in the hot sun.

2.33   Two countries should _____ their fighting.

2.34   Give flavor to your foods by adding _____.

Answer these questions.

2.35   What is the difference between shaft mining and strip mining?

_____

_____

2.36   What is meant when it is said that a mine has "streets?"

_____

_____

 Do this activity.

2.37   Write one sentence telling one good thing about strip
        mining. Then write another sentence telling something
        that is not so good about strip mining.

        a._____

        b._____

A STORY OF ERIC

In this story you will read about Eric. Like many boys his age, Eric wanted to be a miner like his father. In the mining town where Eric lived, boys often grew up to be miners as their fathers had been. A boy would marry a girl from the same mining town. They would raise a family, and their boys might become miners. People felt close to each other. People understood mining ways. A mining town was almost like a big family. People stuck together in times of sadness. They had fun together in happy times. Now read about a day that Eric will not forget.

Eric was waiting. He glanced at his mother. Her head was bowed in prayer. Eric went to the window and looked out to make sure his twin sisters, Carol and Pam, were safe in the backyard.

Just two hours ago all had been well. How could so much have happened in two short hours!

In all the houses in Coalburg, a small mining town in Pennsylvania, mothers and children were quiet—and sad. Their husbands and fathers were in the mine.

At six o'clock that morning, Eric's father had left home for work. Before he went Eric's mother and father had prayed for God's help for all the family.

"But of all the family," prayed Eric, "Daddy needs your help, dear Lord. Please take care of him and bring him out of the mine safely."

Eric loved his father so much. His father was strong and good and worked very hard to make a living for his family.

Children of mining families know the dangers of working in the mine. Mining is safer today. Even so, accidents could still happen.

And an accident had happened.

Two hours ago, Eric's teacher had rung the bells and called the children in early from recess. Sadly, she said, "Children, we are closing school early. There has been trouble in the mine. You must go home and stay with your families and wait for news."

So the children had gone home.

Now, as Eric looked sadly out the window he felt very unhappy. Eric felt that everything looked the same—all the houses, all the children. The world outside looked gloomy black—like coal, like one huge, black rock.

Waiting for News from the Mine

Eric saw in his mind the coal mine—the black coal mine. He thought of the darkness there. He felt he could even smell the coal dust.

The miners were trapped. A prop had fallen. The way out of the mine was blocked.

Then Eric remembered. He remembered a Bible verse he had learned at Sunday school. It was found in Psalm 139:12, "...the night shineth as the day: the darkness and the light are both alike to thee."

Eric felt that there was light in the mine. The light was stronger than a miner's light could ever be. The light came from God.

"Dear Lord, I know you will take care of my daddy. I know you will bring him home safely. Thank you, God," Eric prayed.

Suddenly Eric felt stronger. He knew the Lord would take care of his father and the other trapped men.

Eric turned back from the window and said, "Mother, should we go to the mine?"

"No, Eric, the rescue men have asked us to stay at home. When there is news, the whistle will blow. We can go to the mine then," Eric's mother answered.

It seemed a long time before they heard the whistle, but all along Eric felt that God would protect his father.

Later that evening Eric's father was safely home. He hugged his children and held them close to him.

Late into the night, Eric lay awake. He heard his father talking quietly to his mother, "Even though it was dark, it seemed to me there was a light. I was not afraid."

Eric smiled. Then he prayed, "Thank you, God, for saving my daddy."

Soon Eric was asleep.

In your Bible, find Psalm 139. The verse that Eric remembered came from this Psalm. Read the Psalm with a friend. You read the first verse and your friend the second, each taking turns until you have read the whole Psalm.

2.38   Copy verse 12. Eric remembered this verse.

_____

_____

_____

_____

_____

_____

Study what you have read and done for this Self Test. This Self Test will check what you remember of this part and other parts you have read.

SELF TEST 2

Write true **or** false.

2.01   _____ A cage in a mine is for digging coal.

2.02   _____ Coal was made by people to help heat their houses.

2.03 _____ A coal mine can be as large as a town.

2.04 _____ A miner today is in danger of going blind from poor lighting.

2.05 _____ Peat is formed before coal.

2.06 _____ Shaft mining is done deep in the ground.

2.07 _____ A miner today uses a pick and shovel to mine the coal.

2.08 _____ Mining has changed much over the years.

2.09 _____ Everything that moves or works needs energy.

Draw lines to match the words.

2.010	fuel	fuels
2.011	strip mining	passages into the earth
2.012	tunnels	mining on the surface of the land
2.013	anthracite	hard coal
2.014	coal, gasoline, oil	makes energy

Draw lines to match the danger with new ways of mining.

2.015	poor lighting	steel props
2.016	cave-ins	electric lights
2.017	explosions of gas	a fire boss

Circle the correct answer.

2.018 Shaft mining is _____.

surface   underground   easy

2.019 Coal is _____.

plant   soft   rock

2.020 As well as being a fuel, coal has many _____.

ashes   by-products   colors

EACH ANSWER, 1 POINT

16	
	20

Teacher check _____

Initial   Date

My Score

III. PENNSYLVANIA—THE STATE OF COAL MINES

Pennsylvania is one of the oldest states in the eastern part of the United States. Green hills, rushing rivers, farms, and large cities make it a fine state in which to live. Pennsylvania also has much coal and many mines.

VOCABULARY

bifocals   (bī'fō kuls)   Glasses worn by people who need two different ways to see.

SPECIAL WORDS

Appalachian Mountains	Henry Steigel	Liberty Bell
Benjamin Franklin	Hershey	Minnesota
Betsy Ross	Lake Erie	William Penn
Declaration of Independence	Pennsylvania	Philadelphia
Quakers	Pittsburgh	

Ask your teacher to say these words with you.
Teacher check _____

Initial   Date

THE STATE

Are you ready for a trip through Pennsylvania? Philadelphia is the largest city. Philadelphia means "city of brotherly love." The Quakers who started the city believed that God loved everyone.

Independence Hall is in Philadelphia. In this building is the room where the men signed the Declaration of Independence in 1776. They said that the American colonies wanted to be free from England. The Liberty Bell is there, too.

The house where Betsy Ross made the first American flag is also in Philadelphia. The house is very narrow and tall.

Do this map activity.

3.1   This map of Pennsylvania is for your trip. As you read put the names of the places you visit on the map. Start at Philadelphia. Ask your teacher for a map of Pennsylvania.

Teacher check _____

                    Initial   Date

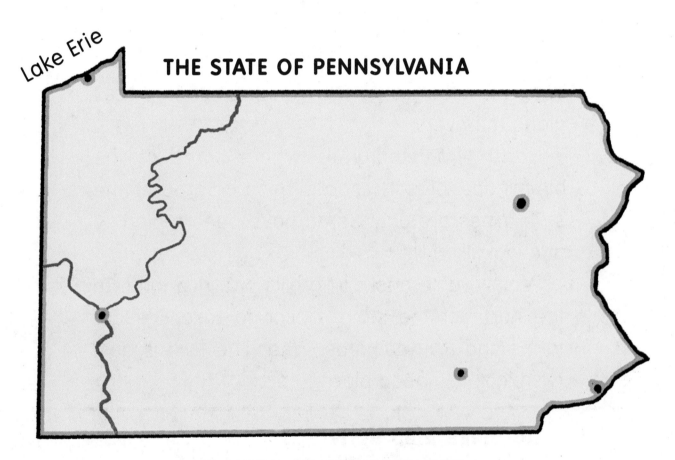

THE STATE OF PENNSYLVANIA

THE STATE OF PENNSYLVANIA

The next town to visit is Hershey. This town is where Mr. Hershey started a chocolate factory years ago. You can smell the candy as you drive into town. The street lights are in the shape of candy, and the streets have candy names.

31 (thirty-one)

The flower gardens are so pretty.

The Pennsylvania Turnpike runs east and west across the state. The turnpike goes across and through the Appalachian Mountains. The tunnels are exciting. The turnpike is a toll road and every car or truck must pay to use it.

Pittsburgh is the second largest city in Pennsylvania. Pittsburgh is famous for its iron and steel mills. The mills were built when there was plenty of coal to fuel the machines. Two rivers meet to form one big river at Pittsburgh. Coal, iron, and steel can be shipped to other places along the rivers.

North of Pittsburgh is where some of the bituminous, or soft coal, is mined. Some of the strip mines are ugly. Some have been replanted and look like hills.

Pennsylvania has rolling hills and rich land. In the north of the state, closer to Lake Erie are farms and fruit orchards. When the fruit is ripe, this place is a good place to be.

Do these map activities.

3.2   You should have the names of towns, a road, and some mountains on your map now. Mark the area of bituminous coal on your map.

3.3   Use another map to see what states are beside Pennsylvania and put their names on your map.

Teacher check _____
                        Initial   Date

The city of Erie is a part of Lake Erie. Ships bring iron ore across the lake from Minnesota. The iron ore will be shipped to Pittsburgh to be used to make steel.

Do these map activities.

3.4   Mark the city of Erie on your map. Draw an ore ship on your map.

3.5   Mark Wilkes-Barre. Put hard coal on your map.

3.6   Many other towns and places can be visited in Pennsylvania. Use another book to discover somewhere else that would be interesting to visit. Mark this place on your map and write three sentences about this place.

_____

_____

_____

_____

Teacher check _____
                        Initial   Date

FAMOUS MEN

The word Pennsylvania means Penn's woods. The state has this name because a man named William Penn received the land from the king of

England. The king owed Penn's father some money. William asked the king to give him land in America to pay him back.

William Penn was a man who loved God. He set up rules for his new colony that would please God. The Indians loved and trusted Penn because he was fair with them. He set up laws that were fair to everyone. He believed that God wanted people to show brotherly love for each other.

Another famous Pennsylvanian was Benjamin Franklin. Benjamin Franklin started the first public library in the American colonies. He found out by flying a kite in an experiment that lightning was really electricity.

Benjamin Franklin

Ben Franklin wrote many fine sayings and words of wisdom. Many of his sayings can be found in his book called <u>Poor Richard's Almanack</u>.

Among his many inventions are the lightning rod, **bifocal** eyeglasses, and the Franklin stove.

Henry Stiegel, a settler from Germany, started making glass in Pennsylvania. He made beautiful vases and bottles in his factory. Today Stiegel's vases and bottles are worth much money.

Many people helped to make Pennsylvania a fine state. These people have been good Americans as well as Pennsylvanians.

Do this activity.

3.7 Here is one of Franklin's famous sayings, "A stitch in time saves nine." Write down what you think this saying means.

_____

_____

_____

_____

Choose the correct answer and circle it.

3.8 The Indians trusted William Penn because _____.

a. Penn had money

b. Penn was fair to the Indians

c. Penn was a friend of the king of England

3.9   Benjamin Franklin _____.

       a. started the first library in America

       b. made vases

       c. gave money to the king

3.10   Henry Stiegel _____.

       a. made silverware

       b. painted pictures

       c. made glassware

3.11   Philadelphia means "city of _____.

       a. motherly need"

       b. brotherly love"

       c. sisterly hope"

3.12   The king of England _____.

       a. gave land to the Indians

       b. gave land to William Penn

       c. built a home in America

3.13   Benjamin Franklin made special glasses called

       _____.

       a. bifocals

       b. brocades

       c. buckskins

Fun Facts to Find

3.14   Use a special book to find the state bird of Pennsylvania. Draw and color the bird. Find out why this bird was chosen.

3.15   Find the state flower of Pennsylvania. Draw and color the flower. Read to learn why they chose this flower.

3.16   Hunt for the picture of the Pennsylvania state flag. Draw and color your picture. Find out how this flag became the state flag.

State Bird	State Flower	State Flag

Teacher check _____
                        Initial   Date

Pennsylvania has many rivers. Everywhere people wanted to cross a river they built a bridge. The letters -dge have the soft sound of j as in the words jelly and jam.

Here are some words that end in dge.

     bridge (brij)   pledge (pledj)

     judge (judj)   budge (budg)

     hedge (hedj)   grudge (gruj)

Write the correct word from the list in each sentence.

3.17   God wants us to forgive others and not hold a

_____ .

3.18   A _____ has been built across the river.

3.19   At school we say the _____ to our country's flag.

3.20   God tells us not to a._____ other people. He will
        be the b. _____ .

3.21   The heavy bucket of coal was hard to _____ .

3.22   The gardener will trim the _____ in the backyard.

Study what you have read and done for this
last Self Test. This Self Test will check what you
remember in your studies of all parts in this
LIFEPAC. The last Self Test will tell you what parts
of the LIFEPAC you need to study again.

SELF TEST 3

Write true **or** false.

3.01   _____   All the coal in the United States is
                        found in Pennsylvania.

3.02   _____   Pittsburgh has large steel mills.

3.03   _____   Gasoline, steel, and coal are fuels.

3.04   _____   Benjamin Franklin wrote Poor Richard's
                        Almanack.

3.05   _____   Bituminous coal is soft coal.

3.06   _____   Six states border Pennsylvania.

Circle the correct answer.

3.07 The glasses Ben Franklin invented were _____.

       too small   plastic   bifocals

3.08 Hershey, Pennsylvania, is a city known for making

       _____.

       coffee   chocolate   corn

3.09 Pennsylvania is in the _____ part of the United States.

       northern   southern   eastern

3.010 The largest city in Pennsylvania is _____.

       Erie   Pittsburgh   Philadelphia

3.011 The Liberty Bell is in _____.

the chocolate factory

Independence Hall

Betsy Ross's house

Write the correct answer.

3.012 William Penn was given land by the king of _____

_____.

3.013 The paper that was written to say that the United
States wanted to be a country by itself is called the
Declaration of _____.

3.014 Henry Stiegel made _____ in his factory.

3.015 The man who wrote Poor Richard's Almanack was

_____.

3.016 Bituminous coal is _____ coal.

3.017 The name of a hard coal is _____.

39 (thirty-nine)

3.018 Mining coal deep in the ground is called _____
_____ .

3.019 A by-product of coal is _____ .

3.020 The walls of mine tunnels are made safer with
_____ .

EACH ANSWER, 1 POINT

16	
	20

Teacher check _____

Initial   Date

My Score

Review
REVIEW
Review

Before taking the LIFEPAC Test, you should do these self checks.

1. _____ Did you do good work on your last Self Test?

2. _____ Did you study again those parts of the LIFEPAC you didn't remember?

   Check one: ☐ Yes (good)

   ☐ No (ask your teacher)

3. _____ Do you know all the new words in "Vocabulary"?

   Check one: ☐ Yes (good)

   ☐ No (ask your teacher)